MYTHS AND TAL
OF THE
AMERICAN INDIA